FAMOUS LATINOS

Diego Rivera

Artist of Mexico

Lila and Rick Guzmán

Enslow Elementary

an imprint of

Enslow Publishers, Inc.

40 Industrial Road
Box 398
Berkeley Heights, NJ 07922
USA

http://www.enslow.com

Series Adviser
Bárbara C. Cruz, Ed.D.
Professor, Social Science Education
University of South Florida

Series Consultant
Allan A. De Fina, Ph.D.
Past President of the New Jersey Reading Association
Professor, Department of Literacy Education
New Jersey City University

Note to Parents and Teachers: The *Famous Latinos* series supports National Council for the Social Studies (NCSS) curriculum standards. The Words to Know section introduces subject-specific vocabulary words.

This series was designed by Irasema Rivera, an award-winning Latina graphic designer.

Enslow Elementary, an imprint of Enslow Publishers, Inc.
Enslow Elementary® is a registered trademark of Enslow Publishers, Inc.

Library of Congress Cataloging-in-Publication Data

Guzmán, Lila, 1952–
    Diego Rivera : artist of Mexico / Lila and Rick Guzmán.— 1st ed.
        p. cm. — (Famous latinos)
    Includes index.
    ISBN 0-7660-2641-8
    1. Rivera, Diego, 1886–1957—Juvenile literature. 2. Painters—Mexico—Biography—
Juvenile literature. I. Rivera, Diego, 1886–1957. II. Guzmán, Rick. III. Title. IV. Series.
    ND259.R5G89 2006
    759.972—dc22   2005031769

Printed in the United States of America

10 9 8 7 6 5 4 3 2 1

To Our Readers: We have done our best to make sure all Internet addresses in this book were active and appropriate when we went to press. However, the author and the publisher have no control over and assume no liability for the material available on those Internet sites or on other Web sites they may link to. Any comments or suggestions can be sent by e-mail to comments@enslow.com or to the address on the back cover.

Every effort has been made to locate all copyright holders of material used in this book. If any errors or omissions have occurred, corrections will be made in future editions of this book.

Illustration Credits:
© 2005 Banco de México Diego Rivera & Frida Kahlo Museums Trust. Av. Cinco de Mayo No. 2. Col. Centro, Del. Cuauhtémoc 06059, México, D.F.:
Instituto Nacional de Bellas Artes y Literatura, p. 25. Photograph © Giraudon/Art Resource, NY, p. 11 (bottom). Photographs © Schalkwijk /Art Resource, NY, pp. 13, 23.

AP / Wide World, pp. 11T, 12, 14, 16T, 17, 20R, 21; Archivo Cenidap-Instituto Nacional de Bellas Artes y Literatura, Mexico City, Mexico, pp. 4R, 10, 16B; Enslow Publishers, p. 4B; Getty Images / Hulton Archive, p. 19; Library of Congress, pp. 7, 8 (both), 18, 20L; Library of Congress, Prints and Photographs Division, Detroit Publishing Company Collection, p. 6; Museo Casa Estudio Diego Rivera y Frida Kahlo/INBA, p. 4T; Time & Life Pictures / Getty Images, pp. 1, 24, 26.

Cover Illustration: Courtesy of Smith College Museum of Art, Northampton, Massachusetts. Diego Rivera, Mexican (1886-1957). Self-Portrait, January 1941. Oil on canvas, stretcher: 24" x 16 7/8" (60.96 x 42.8625 cm). Smith College Museum of Art, Northampton, Massachusetts. Gift of Irene Rich Clifford.

❈ Contents ❈

Diego Rivera

Diego, about four years old.

MEXICO

Tijuana

PACIFIC OCEAN

Guanajuato

Mexico City

Cancun

1

Drawing on the Walls

One day, when Diego Rivera was a little boy, he picked up a pencil and started to draw. He drew on everything: the walls, the doors, and the furniture. To save the house, Diego's father gave him a special room covered with paper. He told Diego he could draw on anything in that room.

For the rest of his life, Diego never stopped drawing. He grew up to become a mural painter, an artist who paints big pictures on the walls of buildings.

Diego was born on December 8, 1886, in Guanajuato (Gwah-nah-HWAH-toh). It is a hilly town

Diego was born in this small town.

in the middle of Mexico. He had a twin brother named Carlos. His parents, María and Diego de Rivera, were both schoolteachers. When Diego was a year and a half old, his twin brother died. Carlos had always been sickly. It was a very sad time for the family.

For the next two years, Diego often stayed with his babysitter, Antonia, in her village in the mountains. At home, he lived in a beautiful house with his mother, father, and two aunts. In 1891, his baby sister, María, was born.

As a child, Diego loved wind-up toys and trains. He was fascinated by the way they worked. He liked going to the train station to watch the trains pull in.

When Diego was almost seven, his family moved to Mexico City. In school, all Diego cared about was drawing. At age ten, he started taking evening classes at Mexico's national school of art, the San Carlos Academy. After a year, he stopped going to regular school. Instead he went to the San Carlos Academy every day.

Diego and his family moved to a busy street like this in Mexico City.

In art school, Diego studied the work of great artists. In the streets of Mexico, he saw a different kind of art. Diego learned a lot from the cartoons drawn by a popular artist, José Guadalupe Posada.

Everyone saw that Diego had a lot of talent. He was one of the best students in the school. He won art contests and graduated from school with high honors. The government gave him a scholarship—an award of money for school—to study art in some European countries. In 1907 Diego left for Europe to learn even more about painting. He was twenty years old.

Diego liked Posada's artwork.

❋ 2 ❋

Becoming a Painter

Diego went to Spain, France, and other countries, studying art, meeting other artists, and painting pictures. He painted landscapes (pictures of the countryside), portraits (pictures of people), and still lifes (pictures of objects, such as fruit and flowers).

In 1910, war broke out in Mexico. Most Mexicans were very poor. They were tired of working for rich people and not owning any land. They believed that a new government would make their lives better. So they began fighting to get rid of President Porfirio Díaz (DEE-ahs). He was a cruel dictator who had ruled

Diego in Spain in 1907.

Mexico for more than thirty years. The war was called the Mexican Revolution. It went on for ten years.

During this time, Diego was in Europe, working on his art. In Paris, France, he met the great artist Pablo Picasso. From Picasso, Diego learned about a kind of art called cubism. A cubist painting does not look like a real person or object. Instead, the painting shows a person or object from the front, back, and sides—all at the same time. The artist paints in shapes, such as squares, circles, and triangles. The Mexican Revolution was the subject of one of Diego's most famous cubist paintings, *Zapatista Landscape* (1915). It shows a Mexican hat, blanket, and gun in front of some trees and mountains.

Emiliano Zapata helped lead the Mexican Revolution.

When Diego returned home in 1921, the war had ended. The new leaders believed that Mexico's art was for all its people. They did not want art to be locked inside museums. So they asked Diego and other artists to paint murals on the walls of public buildings. Diego liked the idea that all people—rich and poor— would be able to enjoy his paintings. He was also happy because the pictures in a mural can tell a story. Many Mexicans did not know how

Zapatista Landscape **is a cubist still life about the revolution.**

Diego's helpers built tall wooden platforms so he could paint the high parts of his murals.

to read. Diego's murals were a way to teach them about Mexico's history and heroes.

In 1922, Diego started his first mural. It was on the walls of the National Preparatory (pree-PAIR-uh-tor-ee) School, one of Mexico's best high schools. Painting a mural was hard work. Sometimes Diego worked for more than twelve hours straight. Sometimes he did not stop to eat. When he painted a mural, the plaster on the wall had to be wet. He had to finish painting before it dried.

People liked to watch Diego work, and he liked to entertain them with stories about his life. Some of the stories were true. Some were tall tales. Diego was famous for his great stories and his wild imagination.

This is part of a mural called *Feast of the Day of the Dead*. Follow the arrow to find Diego's face. It is under the guitar-playing skeleton on the right.

The Mexican government asked Diego to paint murals in the National Palace. On the staircase, Diego painted the history of Mexico. Other walls came alive with the temples, palaces, and gods of Indian tribes in Mexico long ago. On one wall, Diego painted corn, beans, tobacco, chocolate, cotton, tomatoes, peanuts, and chewing gum. He wanted Mexicans to be proud of the products they gave to the rest of the world.

Diego's *History of Mexico* in the National Palace.

3

Murals in the United States

One day while Diego was painting a mural, an eighteen-year-old woman came to see him. She showed him three paintings and asked what he thought of them. He said they were very good. Her name was Frida Kahlo. Diego liked Frida, and he began visiting her at home. Soon, they fell in love. On August 21, 1929, they married.

Diego's fame as an artist was spreading all over the world. When people in the United States heard about his murals in Mexico, they asked him to paint some for them.

Meeting Frida was "the most important fact of my life," said Diego.

In 1930, Diego and Frida packed their bags and went to California. There, he and Frida were treated like movie stars. They went to many parties and met important people. Diego painted a few murals in San Francisco, California. Then he learned that the Museum of Modern Art in New York City wanted to put on a show of some of his paintings. He was thrilled. To Diego, this was the biggest honor of all for an artist. The museum displayed more than a hundred of his paintings. The show was a big success.

Diego was such a big man that he and Frida were often called "the elephant and the dove." This picture was taken on their wedding day.

Next, Diego and Frida went to Detroit, Michigan, a busy city with big factories making cars. All his life, machines fascinated Diego. He loved to watch them move and make noise. For his murals on the walls of the Detroit Institute of Art, he painted people working in the factories with big machines, pipes, and motors.

In 1933 a rich American named John D. Rockefeller asked Diego to paint a mural on a building that his family owned in New York City. This job did not go well.

When Diego painted, he would not let anyone tell him what to do. One day Rockefeller stopped by to

Part of Diego's *Detroit Industry*. He thought machines were very exciting.

see the mural. He was shocked and angry. Diego had added the face of a Russian leader named Vladimir Lenin. Rockefeller did not want Lenin's face in the mural. He told Diego to paint over it. Diego said no. Soon after, Diego was given a message: He must stop working on the mural.

Rockefeller had the unfinished mural covered with paper so no one could see it. A little later, he ordered the mural destroyed. Diego was upset, but he had photographs of his work. When he went back to

Mexico, he painted a copy of the mural on the walls of the Palace of Fine Arts in Mexico City. He kept Lenin's face. Near it, he added Rockefeller's face.

Diego did not want anyone telling him what he could— or could not—paint.

4

Diego and Frida

Sometimes Diego painted his own picture, and sometimes he painted portraits of famous people. He saw beauty and importance in everyone. So he also painted pictures of farmers and other working people. Children were some of his favorite subjects, too.

Diego's wife, Frida, was also a painter, but their work was very different. While he filled huge walls with his art, she

Frida made paintings of herself and her life, like *The Two Fridas* and other pictures hanging on the wall.

painted small portraits of herself. Diego's murals tell big stories about Mexico. Most of Frida's paintings are about things that happened in her own life.

Diego loved his wife very much, but he was not always a good husband. Frida and Diego's marriage had many problems. After ten years, they got a divorce.

In 1940, the city of San Francisco asked Diego to paint a mural about Mexicans and Americans

This photo of Diego and Frida was taken in San Francisco a few days before their second marriage.

working together. Diego liked San Francisco and was happy to go back. For this mural, *Pan-American Unity*, he showed life in both Mexico and the United States. He painted scenes from the past and the present. He included portraits of Mexicans and Americans who worked for freedom. Because Diego loved machines, he put some in the mural. Frida's picture was there as well.

Diego was miserable without Frida. She missed him too. On his birthday, December 8, 1940, Diego and Frida married for the second time. He was fifty-four years old.

✳ 5 ✳

A Mural of Memories

In 1947 a hotel in Mexico City hired Diego to paint a mural in the dining room. Nearby was a wonderful park. Diego remembered trips to the park and all the fun he had there. He decided to do a mural of the park. In *Dream of a Sunday Afternoon in Alameda Park*, he painted a picture of himself as a little boy. He has a frog in one pocket and a snake in another. Diego drew many people from his life and things from his childhood. He put his wife, Frida, in the mural standing behind little Diego. The mural also shows important scenes from Mexican history.

In the middle of this part of *Dream of a Sunday Afternoon in Alameda Park,* look for the young Diego, with Frida standing behind him. A skeleton in a big hat holds Diego's hand. On the other side of the skeleton is the artist José Guadalupe Posada.

Diego's studio was filled with his art.

Diego finished the mural in 1948. The owners of the hotel did not like one part of this mural. They asked Diego to change it. When he said no, they covered the mural with a sheet. Eight years went by before Diego agreed to make the change. Then, at last, people could see this beautiful mural. Today, *Dream of a Sunday Afternoon in Alameda Park* is one of Diego's most famous murals.

In 1949, Diego painted this portrait of himself as an old man. It is called *The Ravages of Time*.

For Diego, art was more important than anything else.

In 1949 the National Institute of Fine Arts put together a special show of Diego's work. He had been painting for more than fifty years. Diego also collected art made by Indians who lived in Mexico long, long ago. He built his own museum, called Anahuacalli (ah-nah-wah-CAH-yee), just for this artwork.

On July 13, 1954, Diego's wife, Frida, died. Three years later, on November 24, 1957, Diego died of heart failure. He was seventy-one years old. He gave his museum to the Mexican people.

Diego is one of the world's great artists. He painted many pictures of all sizes, but he is

"The most joyous moments of my life were those I had spent in painting."

best known for his murals. If all his murals were put side by side, they would cover more than a mile. Diego loved Mexico, and he used his art to show that all Mexicans, rich or poor, were important. His murals told stories of the past and the present. His art taught the Mexican people to be proud of their country.

✳ Timeline ✳

1886 Born in Guanajuato, Mexico, on December 8.

1893 His family moves to Mexico City.

1896 Diego starts going to art school.

1907 Travels to Europe to study art.

1921 Returns to Mexico.

1922 Starts painting his first mural.

1929 Marries Frida Kahlo, who is also an artist.

1930 Diego paints murals in San Francisco.

1931 Museum of Modern Art in New York City has a special show of his work.

1932 Paints murals in Detroit.

1933 Begins painting a mural at Rockefeller Center in New York, but is fired. Returns to Mexico.

1954 Frida Kahlo dies.

1957 Diego dies on November 24.

Words to Know

academy—A school that teaches special subjects, such as art, music, or dance.

dictator—A person who rules with total power.

factory—A place where cars, clothes, or other goods are made.

miserable—Very unhappy.

mural—A large work of art on a wall or ceiling.

museum—A building where people can see works of art and science.

plaster—A paste that hardens and is used to coat walls.

preparatory—To get ready for something. A preparatory school gets students ready for college.

public—Open to everyone.

revolution—Overthrowing the government to put new leaders in place.

tall tales—Stories that are not true.

❋ Learn More ❋

Mattern, Joanne. *Diego Rivera*. Edina, Minn.:
   Abdo, 2005.

Schaefer, Adam R. *Diego Rivera*. Chicago, Ill.:
   Heinemann Library, 2003.

Schoeneberger, Megan. *Diego Rivera: Artist and
   Muralist*. Mankato, Minn.: Capstone Press, 2006.

⚹ Internet Addresses ⚹

"The Virtual Diego Rivera Web Museum."
  <http://www.diegorivera.com>
This site has a biography, pictures of Diego's artworks, and some short videos.

"The Diego Rivera Mural Project,"
City College of San Francisco.
  <http://www.riveramural.com>
See Diego's Pan-American Unity mural and learn more about the artist and about murals.

"American Masters: Diego Rivera."
  <http://www.pbs.org>
On this Web site, type "Diego Rivera" into the search box on the upper right. Then click on "American Masters" to find information about Diego from a public television broadcast.

✻ Index ✻